TREETOPS

Fire in the Dark

Written by David Hunt
and illustrated by Alex Brychta

OXFORD
UNIVERSITY PRESS

OXFORD
UNIVERSITY PRESS

Great Clarendon Street, Oxford OX2 6DP, United Kingdom

Oxford University Press is a department of the University of Oxford. It furthers the University's objective of excellence in research, scholarship, and education by publishing worldwide. Oxford is a registered trade mark of Oxford University Press in the UK and in certain other countries

Text written by David Hunt, based on the original characters created by Roderick Hunt and Alex Brychta

First Edition published in 2012

British Library Cataloguing in Publication Data

Data available

ISBN: 978-0-19-8475699

10 9 8 7 6 5 4 3 2 1

Printed in China by Imago

Paper used in the production of this book is a natural, recyclable product made from wood grown in sustainable forests. The manufacturing process conforms to the environmental regulations of the country of origin.

Acknowledgements: The publisher and authors would like to thank the following for their permission to reproduce photographs and other copyright material:

P46 North Wind Picture Archives/Alamy; Mary Evans Picture Library; Picsfive/Shutterstock; spaxiax/Shutterstock; oriontrail/Shutterstock; **PP46-47** The Print Collector/Alamy; Jakub Krechowicz/Shutterstock; Blaz Kure/Shutterstock; **P47** Interfoto/Sammlung Rauch/Mary Evans; magicinfoto/Shutterstock; Leigh Prather/Shutterstock; Alistair Laming/Alamy; Timewatch Images/Alamy

Chapter 1

No one was in the mood for a madman. It was just too hot.

"Plague! Fire! Famine!" the madman shouted as he strode back and forth through the crowds of people on the bridge. "'Tis 1666 and London is doomed!"

The madman grabbed at passers-by. He had to tell someone. But they always pushed him away. If only someone would listen. But no one would.

On the side of the bridge, a dark man stood still, staring out at the river. "Maybe he will listen!" thought the madman. He weaved his way through the crowds crying, "The end of the world is now!"

Even when the madman stopped next to him, the dark man didn't move. He continued to stare out from the bridge. What was he looking at?

The madman squinted in the bright sunshine. Some way down the river were two tall ships. Their proud masts shimmered in the hazy heat. They were Royal Navy warships. The dark man seemed to be studying them closely.

On the decks of both ships, sailors were busy preparing to go to sea.

The madman tugged at the man's sleeve. "You see! Last year it was the plague. This year we are at war! The end of the world is coming, I tell you."

Slowly, the dark man turned his head and stared into the madman's eyes. The madman felt as if his heart had stopped.

The dark man smiled. "Yes. The end of the world *is* coming!" he whispered.

The madman couldn't believe what he had seen in the other man's eyes. A darkness so terrifying that it sent the madman stumbling away.

A Viran darkness.

The Viran hadn't wanted to reveal himself to anyone. He wasn't ready for that, yet. But then, what did it matter? No one would believe a madman.

The Viran turned back and studied the two ships. He needed to smuggle something on board. That was his deadly task. But how, when the ships were so heavily guarded?

Chapter 2

The madman stumbled through the crowds. He crashed heavily against a hand cart loaded with sacks of flour. It had just come from the mill at the end of the bridge.

The man pushing the cart shouted at him. "Kindly stand aside! I am in a hurry!"

"I've seen the darkness!" cried the madman.

The man driving the cart glanced quickly at the two warships downstream.

"I don't have time for this," he muttered.

"I know you!" cried the madman. "You are that Mr Royal-bread-and-biscuit man!"

"Thomas Farriner, the King's Baker. Supplier of bread and biscuit to his Majesty's Navy, if you please," snapped Thomas. "Though I might not be for much longer, if you don't get out of my way. I have an order of biscuit that has to be finished and on board ship by tomorrow."

As Thomas pushed on through the crowd, the Viran turned and followed. He had heard Thomas talking to the madman, and now he had an idea.

Chapter 3

It was late by the time Thomas had finished baking. As he packed the last of the Navy's order for ship's biscuit, his concentration was broken by a noise outside. It was the night watchman walking up Pudding Lane.

Thomas listened to the watchman's familiar call, "'Tis after one. Take care of your lock, your light and your fire, and then you are done!"

Wearily, Thomas raked out the glowing embers in his oven, put out the candles and went to bed.

Time passed. All was quiet in the narrow lanes and alleys. Not even the occasional chime of church bells disturbed the sleeping city. Then, out of the darkness, two figures crept into Pudding Lane.

"Where are we?" Neena muttered quietly. "Wherever are we?"

They paused as if waiting for an answer. Then Neena spoke again. "Oh, great! I've lost contact. I can't get hold of Tyler."

Most of the buildings in the lane had signs hanging from them. "If they're shops," said Neena, "maybe they'll give us a clue."

But Nadim wasn't listening. He started to run. He had seen something.

Halfway up the lane, one of the shop windows had started to glow with a flickering orange light. As the light grew, Neena could make out the shop's sign. It was a loaf of bread: a baker's sign.

"Neena, quick! Fire!" Nadim was already pushing at the bakery door by the time Neena caught up with him. By chance, the door was unlocked.

Nadim held his breath and pushed his way into the room. The top half of the room was filled with choking smoke. He dropped to the floor and crawled. His skin felt tight from the intense heat. "I don't think there's anyone in here!" he shouted.

"Then get out!" screamed Neena. "Now!"

"No!" shouted Nadim. "I can just make out the fire. It hasn't spread far. I reckon I could put it out."

THOMAS
FARRINER
PUDDING LANE

Without waiting for an answer, Nadim looked around for something to use. To one side was a stack of crates with a heavy canvas cloth thrown over them. Written on the crates were the words, "H.M. Royal Navy – Ship's Biscuit".

With all his strength, Nadim hauled the canvas across the room, and swung it up, over the fire. The cloth smothered the flames in an instant. With the fire out, he staggered out into the lane, coughing.

"You are an idiot!" snapped Neena. "You could have been ..." Suddenly, the Link in her pocket started to whirr. It was Tyler. Part of a download had got through.

DOWNLOAD FROM TYLER

... I repeat: Danger! September 2nd 1666. The night the Great Fire of London started. Keep clear of area known as 'The City'. You must not change history by getting involved with the fire.

Nadim gasped. "You don't think we ...?"

Neena looked up from the Link. "I do," she nodded. "I think we may have just put out the Great Fire of London before it even got started."

Nadim started to panic. "What do we do now? I mean, we've changed history. Which means everything changes from this point onwards. What do we do?"

Moments later, another broken message arrived from Tyler.

DOWNLOAD FROM TYLER

... going on? The TimeWeb has gone crazy. It's hard to describe. Everything is blurred. It's as if the TimeWeb is trying to change its shape. You must ...

"We've got no choice," said Neena. "We are going to have to restart the fire!"

"But we can't do that!" gulped Nadim. "People could get hurt ... Or worse."

"But who knows what terrible things might happen if history is changed forever?" said Neena. "We have to put history back on course."

Neena turned and went into the bakery.

"We don't need Virans," muttered Nadim. "We're doing a pretty good job messing up history on our own."

Chapter 4

"Something isn't right," said Neena. She was standing in the doorway of the bakery.

"You can say that again," mumbled Nadim.

"No. Seriously," whispered Neena. "Can't you feel it?"

"Feel what?" asked Nadim.

"There's just been a fire, right?" said Neena. "And outside it's a warm night."

She paused. “So why is it freezing in here?”

“Virans!” gasped Nadim. “Maybe they started the Great Fire of London.”

“So what do we do now?” asked Neena. “Should we restart the fire or not?”

“No, that won’t be necessary,” came a voice from the shadows. “You’ve just made my task that much easier. I would only have had to put it out myself.” A candle was lit. At the far end of the bakery stood a Viran.

Instantly, Neena and Nadim went for their Zaptraps.

"Fools!" sneered the Viran. "You can't use those Time Runner toys in here. Don't you know that? I'm too close. You'd be hit by the zap as well." He stared into their eyes. "So, Mortlock is pinning his hopes on you, is he? You? Pathetic!"

Nadim and Neena's legs were locked solid. They felt dizzy with fear. How did this Viran know so much?

"You have been lucky so far," continued the Viran, as he fixed them with his terrible gaze. "My congratulations! But you have interfered with our work too much."

He lit another candle. "I think you'll find things are not going to be so easy from now on."

The Viran's eyes held both of them. Not only could Neena not move, she was even finding it hard to think.

She felt as if the Viran was looking right inside her head. It was as if he was undoing her memory.

Neena decided she had to take control of her mind before the Viran did. She had to think of something, and quickly. All she could think of was a stupid old nursery rhyme.

"London's burning, London's burning, Fetch the engine! Fetch the engine! Fire! Fire!" she chanted, over and over, in her head.

The Viran cocked his head to one side and looked curiously at her. It was as if he could hear her thoughts. He began to laugh.

"No, no. I'm not here to burn London down. My task is much more interesting than that."

He pulled forward an enormous sack. "This," he said, "is why *I'm* here!"

Neena thought she might be seeing things. The sack was moving on its own. Something inside it writhed and wriggled. Was her mind playing tricks on her?

The Viran opened the sack. "This is the answer," he hissed, pulling out a fistful of squirming legs, tails, black fur, teeth and claws. "Rats!" he laughed. "Plague rats!"

Chapter 5

Neena felt exhausted by the Viran's draining stare, and she was fighting to stay focused. She glanced at Nadim. He seemed to be in a dream.

The Viran held a couple of rats in front of Neena. "You may be wondering why I am here, in this bakery," he sneered. "After all, I could release the rats anywhere in the city and the disease would spread."

"Then ... why?" Neena managed to mutter.

"Perhaps I needed to put out the fire first?" smiled the Viran. "Certainly the Great Fire would have destroyed all my little plague carriers. But then, you've very kindly put it out for me."

"Why ... you ... here?" stuttered Neena.

The Viran wrenched open a crate of ship's biscuit. "Spreading plague in a city just seemed too easy. Almost boring. No. My plan is much more interesting."

He dropped some rats into the crate. "Imagine every ship in the Royal Navy out at sea." He closed the crate and opened another. "Hungry sailors call for their ship's biscuit," he laughed, throwing rats in the next crate. "The crate is opened and the rats escape. Then they begin their terrible work. Plague on board! His Majesty's Navy destroyed, without an enemy warship in sight."

The Viran worked quickly, putting rats in each and every one of the crates of ship's biscuit. When the work was done he paused, picking up the sack.

"It seems I have some left over," he sniggered. "I may as well let them go." He held open the sack. "Go! Go, my pretty ones!"

Neena held her breath. Every fibre in her body was telling her to run, yet she couldn't move.

From the sack, a great tide of rats surged into the room. "There's no way the Time Runners will be able to stop this one," the Viran cackled.

He stared at Neena. "I will not destroy your mind this time. Instead, I want you to go and tell Mortlock. Tell him it is the Virans' turn now!" At that, he left.

For a few minutes, neither Neena nor Nadim could move. Rats scrabbled up the walls and over everything.

It was only the smell of smoke that brought Neena to her senses. In the scramble, a rat had knocked over the candle. It fell into a basket of dry kindling and wood shavings, which burst into flame.

Neena grabbed Nadim. "We have to get out of here, and now!"

Neena and Nadim staggered into the lane. Within seconds the bakery was an angry storm of fire and swirling smoke. The whole building seemed to scream as ancient wooden beams burst into flame.

Above the noise Neena could hear voices. It was the baker, Thomas, and his family. They were climbing out of a top window to safety.

Nadim, still dazed by the Viran, looked up at them. "Fly away home," he muttered. He sounded like a little boy. "House is on fire and all is gone."

"Come on, Nadim," said Neena. "We need to clear our heads."

Chapter 6

The fire in Pudding Lane quickly took hold. The timber houses with their dry, thin walls were no match for the flames. The buildings were so cramped together that the fire spread easily in every direction.

As the fire spread through the streets, the people of London began to panic. Some fled, dragging their possessions with them. Others stayed and tried to fight the fire. But leather buckets filled with waste water could make little difference.

Many people were faced with a stark choice. Let their homes burn, or tear them down using fire-hooks. The hope was to break the fire's progress by making gaps in the tightly packed maze of lanes and alleys. Such drastic action might save the city. But it was such a tough decision that most people hesitated until it was too late.

Chapter 7

To make matters worse, a strong wind served to fan the flames further. Showers of sparks drifted widely over the city. Very soon, fires were breaking out everywhere.

Nadim and Neena were escaping from the fire when Tyler's download arrived.

DOWNLOAD FROM TYLER

Great news! The TimeWeb has settled down. I was trying to sort it, without much luck. Then all of a sudden it just went back to normal!

"I bet that was when the fire started. History's back on track," said Neena.

"Great," said Nadim. "A city's on fire and we're meant to feel good about it."

"Look on the bright side," said Neena. "At least the Viran's plan is finished."

"Unless the plague rats flee the fire like everyone else," added Nadim.

Neena looked at the huge orange glow over the city. "But where would the rats flee to?" she said.

Thousands of flakes of ash were falling from the sky like strange snow. A voice in the distance cried, "It's the end of the world!" They watched as men rushed past carrying buckets of water from the river.

"The river!" said Nadim. "That has to be the safest place right now. Let's go!"

The river was in chaos. The fire had destroyed everything in its path, and now it threatened London Bridge. People, animals, rats – all streamed towards the river's edge. Now, the only escape from the flames was to jump into the muddy water itself. Downstream, the Navy's ships hadn't stirred. They were unable to help. The tide was too low. Only one dark figure stood waiting and watching. It was the Viran.

From every gully and drain, rats scurried from the advancing fire. Among them stood the Viran. Every now and then he bent down and scooped one up. It was as if he were choosing the ones he wanted. The ones carrying plague, perhaps?

Suddenly a flash of blue flame filled the air around the Viran.

The flame hadn't come from the great fire. It had come from Nadim's zaptrap, but he'd missed.

The Viran grinned. He turned and ran through the fire that now licked around the start of the bridge.

"We have to stop him!" shouted Nadim. Grabbing hold of Neena's hand, he plunged into the smoke and flame, after the Viran. Beyond this point, the bridge was still safe but strangely deserted. At the far end was a gatehouse. The Viran ran towards it. But the gates were closed. The Viran was trapped.

Thinking fast, the Viran spun round and smashed his way into the nearest building on the bridge. A flour mill!

Inside the mill was a mass of machinery. Giant cogs, wheels and shafts. Lit by the glare of a thousand fires, it cast strange patterns of shadow and light all around. Being of darkness, the Viran slipped easily into shadows.

It was hard for Nadim and Neena to adjust their eyes to the gloom. All was still. “I can’t see him!” hissed Nadim. With the background roar of the great fire they’d never hear him, either.

In a deadly game of cat and mouse, the Viran moved from one shadow to another around them. “I’m scared,” said Neena.

“Sshh!” whispered Nadim. “Stay absolutely still.” He had had an idea.

Neena gripped her Zaptrap. At Nadim's feet were sacks of flour. Slowly he bent down and grabbed two large handfuls. He threw them as hard as he could in a high arc across the room. A fine dust filled the air, and hung like a strange mist all around.

"Watch for any movement in the dust," Nadim whispered.

Then, to one side, the dust rippled. The air had been disturbed. The Viran had moved.

"Duck!" whispered Neena to Nadim as she launched her Zaptrap. The blue zap reached out towards the Viran. It burst into raw energy. For a fraction of a second the whole space was lit up as millions of particles of flour dust ignited.

The Zaptrap fell to the floor, empty. But the Viran was gone.

"We've used both Zaptraps," said Neena. "We'll have to head back to the Time Vault."

Meanwhile, somewhere down on the river, a small whirlwind of sparks spun over the water. The Viran began to take form again.

Glossary

biscuit *(page 9)* Sometimes called hardtack. A hard dry biscuit made from flour, water and salt. Used during long sea voyages because it did not go bad. *"Supplier of bread and biscuit to his Majesty's Navy, if you please!"*

famine *(page 3)* A serious shortage of food resulting in many starving. *"Plague! Fire! Famine!"*

fire-hooks *(page 33)* A hook on a long pole. Fire-hooks were used to pull down thatch and timber to stop fire spreading. *Let their homes burn, or tear them down using fire-hooks.*

kindling *(page 30)* Small pieces of wood used to start a fire. *The candle fell into a basket of dry kindling and wood shavings, which burst into flame.*

night watchman *(page 10)* It was the job of the watch to patrol the streets at night to protect the sleeping citizens from any dangers, especially criminals and fire. *It was the night watchman walking up Pudding Lane.*

scurried *(page 36)* Ran with short, quick steps. *From every gully and drain, rats scurried from the advancing fire.*

Thesaurus: Another word for ...

scurried *(page 36)* scampered, scrabbled, scuttled.

Tyler's Mission Report

Location:	Date:
London, England.	1666
Mission Status:	**Viran Status:**
Unsuccessful/case open.	1 zapped. NOT trapped.

Notes: Viran still loose. We may have to return.

For the people who lived and worked in London's crowded streets, the Fire was like the end of the world. So many people homeless, lost. Makes me shudder. It was on those same streets that I lived. London had been rebuilt by then. All the buildings were stone, and everything was designed to prevent fire spreading so disastrously, ever again. Weird ... The streets I knew, the walls I climbed, the cellars I hid in, were all there because of that fire. Talking of cellars ... One cellar I remember had a black band of soot running all the way round the walls. 'From the Great Fire,' I was told. Even today, dig down anywhere in London, and you'll find soot.

One good thing, though. The fire destroyed so many rats, London was finally free of the plague.

Sign off: ....Tyler........................

History: downloaded!

The Great Fire of London 1666

With a firestorm hot enough to melt glass and metal, nothing survived the terrible events of September 1666. The city, its buildings, its treasures, its history, all burned to a crust of black lifeless earth.

Once a fire took hold, it was almost impossible to stop it spreading. The buildings, crammed together along narrow lanes, were all made of wood, much of it painted with tar. Even the plaster, mixed with horsehair, spread the fire onwards. The lanes themselves became deadly wind tunnels, drawing whirlwinds of superheated air, which fanned the flames deep into the city.

London had had great fires before, but this fire, at the end of a long hot summer, was the most ferocious of them all.
Out of control for four days, and destroying over 13,500 buildings, it truly was the Great Fire of London.

Sparks were carried across the city on the high winds, and fires seemed to break out everywhere. Many people thought that London was under attack from enemy spies. The bakery in Pudding Lane (where the fire started in reality) was not the first suspect.

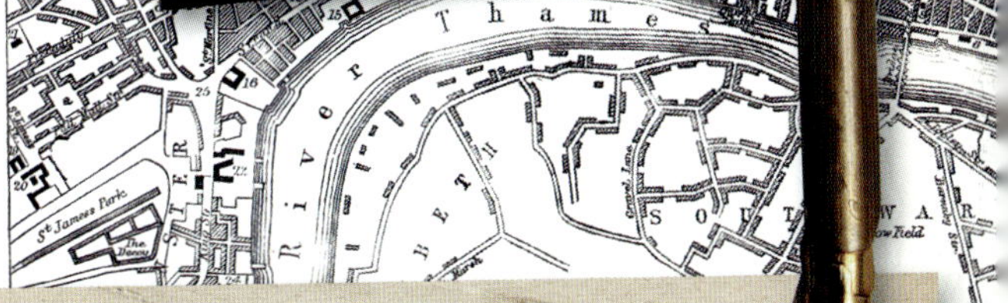

For more information, see the Time Chronicles website:
www.oxfordprimary.co.uk/timechronicles

A voice from history

Last summer, it was plague rather than fire that raged through our streets, burning people up in a feverish black death. If it were a fire, we'd have torn down any house in its path, to try to stop it spreading further. To stop the plague, we tried something similar ...

Desperate measures! At the first sign of illness, poor wretches were locked in their homes with the rest of their family. The door was only unlocked again to pull out the bodies using a long hook. Sounds hard? We had to stop the plague spreading somehow. Besides, once the plague got hold no doctor could help anyway. Oh they tried, with their 'remedies' they called 'waters'. But no amount of 'water' could extinguish the flames that burnt up a victim's insides.

We were terrified.

Isn't it ironic? We even tried setting London alight. By September 1665 fires smoldered everywhere, day and night. The choking smoke, we hoped, would drive this pestilence from our doors. It didn't.